A CHRISTMAS TREE ON VACATION

Written by
Sofia Leon

Illustrated by
Kasia Jakubowska

BLESSINGHAM PRESS

Lily the Christmas tree, oh so green and fully grown,
Stood lonely on the farm, with no family to take her home.

She dreamed of shining bright, with ornaments and lights,
Instead, she'd be alone, all alone on Christmas night.

A tree farm worker saw her sadness and said with a smile,
"Cheer up, dear Lily, you've got time off now for a while.

You have a whole year to spend as you please,
To travel the world, to create memories."

TREE FARM

Lily was hesitant, as she had never left her farm before,
But the thought of adventure made her heart soar.

So she packed her bags and set off to explore,
The wonders of the world and so much more.

W7847

January in Greece, *with* the **Acropolis** so grand,
Lily felt a sense of awe as she strolled that hallowed land.

February in Italy, *where* the **Colosseum** stood tall,
The marks of the past, monuments big and small.

March in France, with the **Eiffel Tower** so high,
Lily felt renewed by the love in the sky.

In April, she arrived in the **UK** by plane,
To see **Buckingham Palace**, where the royal family reign.

May in Egypt, with the **Pyramids** standing tall with grace,
Lily experienced the magic of that ancient place.

June in India, she visited the **Taj Mahal**,
A symbol of love that filled her heart and soul.

July in China, she climbed the **Great Wall**,
A marvel of engineering that can never fall.

In August in Australia, she saw such a sight,
The famous **Sydney Opera House** in the daytime light.

In September in Peru, she visited **Machu Picchu**,
An ancient city, hidden in the Andes under skies so blue.

In October in the USA, she visited **New York City,**
To see the **Statue of Liberty** standing tall and pretty.

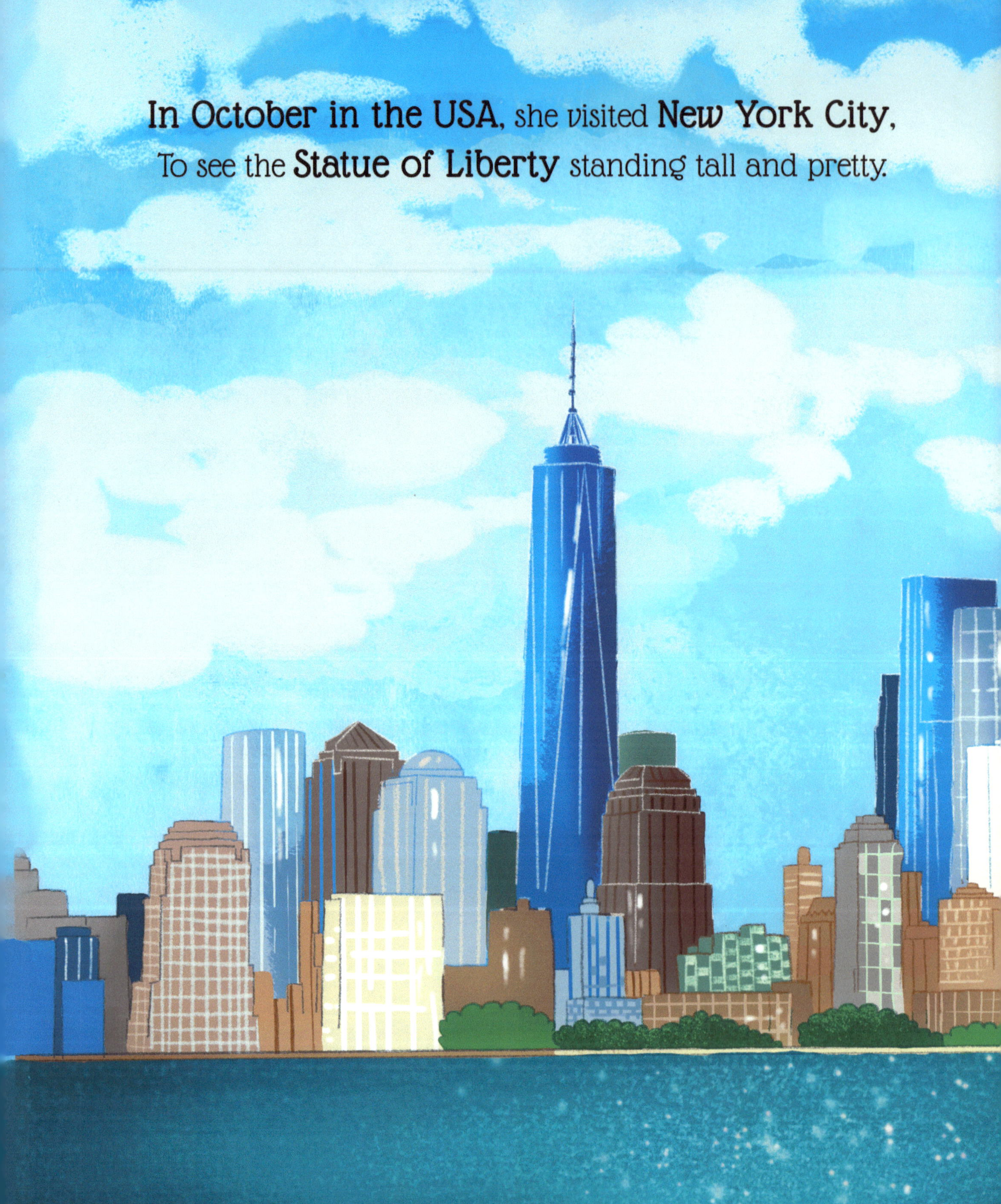

In November in Brazil, she walked on the sand,
On **Copacabana Beach**, where she heard a samba band.

In December, back home she came,
To celebrate Christmas, but it was not the same.

Lily's adventure had filled her with glee,
She had seen so many things and learned so much, you see.

Amidst the trees, a family did appear,
Two children smiling ear-to-ear, their parents full of cheer.

Lily caught their eye with a joyful gleam,
And the family knew she was the tree of their dreams.

They decorated her with baubles and lights,
And put gifts underneath to make the season bright.

The energy within her was bursting at the seams,
Her needles were glowing like the sun's beams.

Lily had found happiness, love, and a family to call her own.
By following her passion, she found her way home.

Written by Sofia Leon
Illustrated by Kasia Jakubowska

Date of production: 2023
Published in the United Kingdom

www.ingramcontent.com/pod-product-compliance
Lightning Source LLC
LaVergne TN
LVHW071224160826
845679LV00003B/896
* 9 7 8 1 7 3 9 3 7 9 9 8 8 *